Dance

Tap and Jazz

Nikki Gamble

H www.heinemann.co.uk/library
Visit our website to find out more information about **Heinemann Library** books.

To order:
☎ Phone 44 (0) 1865 888066
▤ Send a fax to 44 (0) 1865 314091
▢ Visit the Heinemann Bookshop at www.heinemann.co.uk/library to browse our catalogue and order online.

First published in Great Britain by Heinemann Library, Halley Court, Jordan Hill, Oxford OX2 8EJ, part of Pearson Education.
Heinemann is a registered trademark of Pearson Education Ltd.

Editorial: Sarah Shannon and Kate deVilliers
Design: Steve Mead and Geoff Ward
Picture Research: Melissa Allison
Production: Duncan Gilbert

Originated by Modern Age
Printed in China by Leo Paper Group

ISBN 978 0 431 93309 2
12 11 10 09 08
10 9 8 7 6 5 4 3 2 1

British Library Cataloguing in Publication Data
Gamble, Nikki
  Tap and Jazz. – (Dance)
  793.3
A full catalogue record for this book is available from the British Library.

Acknowledgements
The publisher would like to thank the following for permission to reproduce photographs:
©Alamy Images (Photos 12) p. **39**; ©Corbis pp. **12** (Hulton-Deutsch Collection), **18** (Stephanie Methven/Lebrecht Music & Arts), **26** (Bettmann), ©Getty Images pp. **6** (Jacob Silberberg), **10** (Frank Driggs Collection), **11** (Frank Driggs Collection), **13** (Gaston Paris/Roger Viollet), **16** (Peter Stackpole/Time Life Pictures), **37** (CBS Photo Archive), **43** (Sean Gallup); ©Kobal Collection pp. **28** (Warner Bros.), **29** (20th Century Fox), **31** (MGM), **33** (Mirisch-7 Arts/United Artists), **34** (20th Century Fox/Columbia); ©Lebrecht Musics & Arts Library p. **14**; ©Mary Evans Picture Library (Steve Rumney) p. **9**; ©PA Photos (AP Photo) p. **5**; ©Pedro Brenner p. **4**; ©Peter Newark's Americana Library p. **8**; ©Philip Glaser p. **42**; ©Rex Features pp. **20–21** (Ray Tang), **25** (CSU Archives/Everett Collection), **35** (Alastair Muir), **41** (Alastair Muir); ©Topfoto (ullsteinbild) p. **23**.

Cover photograph reproduced with permission of ©Corbis (Michael Walls).

Disclaimer
All the Internet addresses (URLs) given in this book were valid at time of going to press. However, due to the dynamic nature of the Internet, some addresses may have changed, or sites may have changed or ceased to exist since publication. While the author and publishers regret any inconvenience this may cause readers, no responsibility for any such changes can be accepted by either the author or the publishers. It is recommended that adults supervise children on the Internet.

Contents

Some words are printed in bold, **like this.** You can find out what they mean by looking in the glossary, on page 46.

The jazz dance family

Jazz dance began in the early 20th century in the United States, at the same time as jazz music. It was influenced by jazz music's **syncopated** rhythms. Throughout the history of jazz dance, developments in music and dance have gone hand-in-hand.

The term 'jazz dance' covers a huge range of dance styles. It can be **percussive**, like tap dance and stomp, or expressive and **lyrical.** So while it is easy to recognise ballet or ballroom dance, the range of dances called 'jazz' might seem to be unconnected. However, all jazz dance styles share the same roots and essential elements: syncopation, individual style and **improvisation.**

▼ In this contemporary jazz theatre production, the male dancer displays 'jazz hands'. This typical jazz dance gesture with hands open, palms facing forward, and splayed fingers may originate from Al Jolson's performance in *The Jazz Singer* (1927).

These are the winners in a weekly mambo dance contest held at the Savoy Ballroom in Harlem, New York in 1953.

Different jazz dance styles

Styles under the jazz dance umbrella include:

- Popular dance. This is a family of dance styles including street dance, and the dances that developed in the ballrooms and dance halls. Lindy hop and street fusion are part of this family.
- Jazz dance for musical theatre. This was developed because the new musicals of the 20th century featured dance and song routines. These required a more relaxed dance style than formal ballet, so musical theatre led to the birth of jazz technique and the formation of jazz dance classes.
- Concert jazz dance. It is performed by dance companies in a similar way to ballet and modern dance. It developed from the birth of formal jazz technique and musical theatre.

Jazz dance is flexible, versatile, and never stops evolving. Today, jazz dance blends world dance styles such as Latin and Russian dance with essential jazz ingredients.

Jazz dance opportunities

Jazz and tap dance are popular with young people. You can see different styles of jazz and tap dance in many West End and **Broadway** musicals, or in classic films such as *Singin' in the Rain* or *Hellzapoppin'*. You can try jazz and tap for yourself at one of the many dance classes offered by local dance schools or fitness centres. There are also many videos and DVDs especially produced for young people, which demonstrate jazz and tap dance techniques.

The early days of jazz dance

Modern jazz and tap dance have common roots that can be traced back to the dance traditions of African slaves transported to America in the 17th century. The stylization of contemporary black dance reveals the African influence on the dance. The term used to describe the styles and traditions that emerged from the 1600s onwards is 'African-American **vernacular** dance'.

Slaves were taken from many different ethnic groups, each with its own dances. However there were some common features: bent knees, elbows, hips, and ankles. The term 'get down' refers to the bent posture produced by bending at the waist and knees, to bring the body low to the ground. One slave song called on dancers to 'Gimmee de knee bone bent'. This stance reflected a spiritual attitude, which was associated with life and energy.

▼ Contemporary jazz dance has clear African roots. Its characteristics include flat footwork, bent elbows, knees, hips, and ankles. These dancers are in Ghana, West Africa.

In most cases, slaves were not permitted to openly display their culture. Consequently, dance forms started to appear that merged African rhythms and style with European dances. In times of adversity, dance symbolized freedom and lifted the spirits.

Cakewalk

The cakewalk evolved in the late 19th century, from an African American parody of the European style ballroom dances. The name came from the competitions that were organized by the slave owners, for which the winning couple were offered slices of **hoecake**. The dance used traditional African dance steps with exaggerated movements that mimicked the upper classes. It was performed by couples linking arms at the elbows and following an alternating sequence of short hopping steps with high kicking steps. Canes were hung over arms and large bow-ties, top hats and oversize suits were worn by the men.

Dancing became a popular form of entertainment. African American dancers shuffled and jigged at the travelling **medicine shows** and on the showboats. Speciality dances often formed the pre-show entertainment at carnivals, **gillies** and circuses.

Ragtime

Ragtime was a **precursor** to early jazz and is generally thought to be the first American musical genre. It is characterized by its **syncopated** beat. Popular between 1899 and 1918, ragtime began as popular dance music. It developed from black band music and combined characteristics of African folk and European classical music.

The turkey trot

One famous dance of the ragtime era was the turkey trot, which became popular between 1900 and 1910. This fast dance was often performed to ragtime composer Scott Joplin's 'Maple Leaf Rag'. The basic movements include a fast marching **one-step**, with the arms pumping at the side, and occasionally flapping. A famous performance of the dance was given by ballroom dancers Vernon and Irene Castle in the 1913 **Broadway** show, *The Sunshine Girl*. The turkey trot was disapproved of by upstanding members of society, and denounced as immoral by the Pope on the grounds of 'indecent' movements.

▲ The composer Scott Joplin created fast-paced music to which people could dance the turkey trot.

The foxtrot

By 1914, the turkey trot had fallen out of favour. It was replaced by the more elegant foxtrot. Originally danced to ragtime music, the foxtrot was named after its inventor, the **vaudeville** actor Harry Fox. It was first performed in the *Jardin de Danse* on the roof of the New York Theatre.

The foxtrot is a **two-step** dance with a broken (rather than even) rhythm, described as a slow-slow-quick-quick-slow. The foxtrot consists of long walking movements with a rise and fall, and turns. 'On the spot' foxtrot steps were also developed, so that the dance could be enjoyed in halls where there were large numbers of dancers.

▲ These two French dancers are performing the turkey trot.

Dance Facts

The Ziegfeld Follies 1907–31
The Ziegfeld Follies opened in July 1907 on a small garden stage at the top of the New York Theatre. It included elements of high-class vaudeville and was a forerunner of the Broadway show. The show was a spectacular combination of costume and dance. There were up to six wardrobe changes in one evening.

The Follies was famed for its chorus line known as the Ziegfeld Girls.

Before *The Follies* chorus girls were anonymous, but Ziegfeld turned them into celebrities. Many future dance stars, such as Barbara Stanwyck and Paulette Goddard, started out in Ziegfeld's chorus line.

The Follies were the subject of two films, *The Great Ziegfeld* and *Zeigfeld Follies*, starring the tap dancing greats, Fred Astaire, Gene Kelly and Judy Garland.

Jazz music and jazz bands

Jazz music and jazz dance developed together: changes in music influenced dance styles, and the dancers in turn inspired the musicians. New Orleans was the birthplace of jazz music and in the late 19th century it was a lively city, where music, song and dancing were an essential part of life.

Brass bands and jazz bands

At first, jazz music was played by brass bands, which had reached the height of their popularity by 1880. These bands gradually developed into jazz bands in the early decades of the 20th century.

By the beginning of the 20th century, jazz music was spreading across the United States. King Oliver's Creole Jazz Band was based in Chicago. It was one of the best and most influential bands of the day. Oliver played the cornet, and in 1922 he invited Louis Armstrong to play second cornet in the band. Armstrong accepted. It was an electric mix and the audiences eagerly flocked to hear the band.

▼ King Oliver's Creole Jazz Band played in working class dance halls and at high society venues.

▲ Big bands combined elements of ragtime, black spirituals, blues, and European music, and influenced the development of jazz dance. This is Cab Calloway and his Orchestra in 1937.

The big band

In the 1920s, the big band emerged as the most popular arrangement for dance music. Bands had up to 25 musicians playing saxophones, trumpets and trombones, and also included a rhythm section. The music played by the big bands was carefully arranged and written down as sheet music.

Sweet jazz

At this time the most popular dance music was called 'sweet jazz'. The musicians played a soft and romantic melody, accompanied by singing. The music was carefully worked out beforehand, and so the dances also had worked-out steps and sequences. This would change later with the introduction of the swing band, when a more **improvised** style would emerge in dance and music.

Dance Facts

The Cotton Club
The Cotton Club was a famous jazz club in New York. It was where many of the jazz greats played, and an inspiration for musicians and dancers alike. Duke Ellington, Count Basie, Bessie Smith, Cab Calloway and Louis Armstrong were among the finest musicians who played there. The famous **flash dancers**, The Nicholas Brothers, delighted audiences at the Cotton Club with their impressive routines.

Early swing

Swing is a term used to describe a group of dances that were developed to go with the jazz music of the 1920s, 1930s and 1940s. The early swing dances, emerging from the **Dixieland jazz** tradition of New Orleans, USA, included the Charleston and the black bottom.

▲ This flapper girl is dancing the Charleston.

The Charleston

The Charleston was developed in the African American communities in the United States at the beginning of the 20th century. It became popular after it was seen in the **Broadway** musical *Runnin' Wild* in 1923. It was a high tempo dance in which fast, hopping steps were combined with contrasting slower, dragging steps, accompanied by swaying arm movements and **improvisation**.

In the 1920s, the Charleston became popular with **flapper** girls, who danced solo. This was very daring for the time, as it was more conventional to dance with a partner. The solo Charleston was not popular for very long, but it was influential: it developed into a variety of Charleston styles, including partner Charleston, tap Charleston and the lindy hop, which remains popular today.

The black bottom

The Charleston was quickly superseded by the black bottom. The black bottom was also first danced in New Orleans. When it was performed in the show *Dinah* in New York it became an overnight sensation.

The black bottom is a solo dance, and is danced on the **off-beat.** It features bottom slapping and rhythmic arm and hip movements. A famous performance of the black bottom featured in the show *George White Scandals*, in 1926.

Famous Dancers

Josephine Baker became the most popular entertainer in France.

Josephine Baker (1906–75)

Known affectionately as 'The Black Pearl' and 'Black Venus', Josephine Baker was greatly admired for her beauty and sensational dancing. At the height of her career she was showered with gifts and received hundreds of proposals of marriage, but her humble beginnings were a far cry from the celebrity status she achieved.

Born in St Louis, Missouri on 3 June 1906, Baker joined the **vaudeville** theatre when she was 13. In the 1920s, she appeared in the Broadway revues *Shuffle Along* and *Chocolate Dandies*, where she performed as the last dancer in the chorus line. This role was traditionally performed in a comic manner, as if the dancer could not remember the steps. In the final scene the steps are performed perfectly, with the addition of even more complex steps.

Baker's real success came when she moved to Paris, where her performances in *La Revue Nègre*, in which she danced a very lively Charleston, and *La Folie du Jour* assured her position as the most popular entertainer in France. She was saddened by the fact that she never achieved the same success in her native America.

The lindy hop

As the Charleston developed from a solo to a partnered dance, it evolved into different styles, including the lindy hop. The lindy hop started at The Savoy Ballroom, Harlem, where the improvised jazz music suited the style developed by the inventive dancers. According to the popular story, it was named after the famous aviator Charles Lindbergh, who had the nickname 'Lucky Lindy'. When Lindbergh made a solo non-stop flight from New York to Paris in 1926, the newspapers carried the headline 'Lindy hops the Atlantic', and so the dance was named. It is rather misleading, as there is no hopping at all in the dance.

▲ Impressive aerial moves were introduced by lindy hoppers in the 1930s and 1940s.

In 1935, Herbert 'Whitey' White formed a lindy hop group of top dancers at the Savoy Ballroom, so turning **social dance** into performance dance. The dancers practised at The Savoy during the day and performed at society parties at night.

In the 1940s, the swing craze was at its height and film studios began to include swing dance scenes in Hollywood films. Dean Collins was one of the most filmed lindy hoppers and he developed the Hollywood style of lindy hop. He appeared in more than 30 films, including the legendary *Hellzapoppin'*. One of the main differences between the two styles was the swingout: in the Hollywood style, this was straight to the side; in the Savoy style the swingout was circular.

Famous Dancers

'Shorty' George Snowden (1904–unknown)

George Snowden was an early lindy hopper who was just five feet tall. 'Shorty' used his lack of height to advantage by including comic routines that exaggerated his closeness to the ground. His partner Big Bea was much taller then he was and would often carry 'Shorty' off stage at the end of a routine. The crowd loved it. Snowden was dubbed 'The King of the Savoy', and was the only lindy hopper to have a dance step, 'The Shorty George', named after him.

Technique

Basic moves

Lindy hop is a partnered dance with a leader and a follower. The two basic moves of lindy hop are the swingout and the Charleston.

- The swingout is the defining dance move of lindy hop. It is an **eight-count** move that usually starts and ends in open position, with the partners standing apart and facing inwards or outwards, holding one or both hands or standing independently. After the swingout, each dancer improvises alone.

- The Charleston is an eight-count move that usually starts and ends in a closed position, with the partners holding each other while facing towards each other.

A famous lindy hop step is the airstep invented by Frankie Manning, one of the greatest lindy hoppers of all time. In this impressive move, the dancer's partner starts on the dancer's back, is flipped over his head and lands on the ground.

The swing bands

During the 1930s, an exciting new swing style broke on to the dance scene. In 1935, Benny Goodman and his band performed new, **improvised** music: the crowd erupted. It was the birth of a new dance craze – the **jitterbug**.

The four-beat, foot-tapping rhythm replaced the earlier two-beat jazz and was an immediate success. The new relaxed music style led to the reorganization of bands, with more improvisation from the bigger brass and wind sections. This in turn led to an energetic improvised dance style, with lots of spins and underarm turns.

▶ During World War II, about 2 million American troops were stationed in Britain. They brought their dances with them, and the jitterbug became established as a popular dance in Europe.

Swing dances

In the 1930s and 1940s, swing flourished and there were many swing dances, with different cities in the United States having their own unique dances. Swing dances follow either a six- or **eight-count** pattern.

The popularity of the ballrooms opened up new business opportunities for dance teachers. Arthur Murray was the first to sell dance steps by mail. Murray devised a way of teaching dances using footprints, and these were sent out to subscribers lesson by lesson.

Glenn Miller (1904–44)

Orchestra leader Glenn Miller was one of the best known names of the 1940s swing band era. His orchestra emphasized the reed section, so that the clarinet held the melody and was supported **harmonically** by the tenor saxophones. The result was a distinctive sound that was instantly recognizable. During the war years, Glenn Miller's band played at the US bases in Britain. Forces and locals jived the night away. Lyrics for Glenn Miller tunes such as 'Doin' the Jive' illustrate the close connection between music and dance:

> You clap your hands
> And you swing out wide
> Do the susie q
> Mix in a step or two
> Put 'em all together
> And you're doin' the jive

Famous Dances

Swing dances

- The Balboa originated in the Balboa Peninsula region of Newport Beach, California. It was an eight-count dance with intricate footwork. Dance partners used a **close hold**, which suited the crowded dance floors of the Californian ballrooms. The Balboa was usually danced to fast jazz music, and because of its complex footwork it was considered a spectator dance.

- The collegiate shag was danced with a close hold to a two-beat rhythm and combined a variety of slow steps followed by a quick-quick rhythm.

- The St Louis shag was very fast and bouncy. It was usually danced in the closed position, although sometimes partners danced side by side. Steps for this dance follow the sequence: rock step, kick forward, step down, kick forward (other leg), stag step, stomp. For the stag step the leg is lifted with the knee bent. A stomp is a very heavy step, similar to stamping.

Tap dance and vaudeville

The United States is the home of tap dance, which evolved from African dance, Irish step dancing and Lancashire clogging.

English, Irish and African influences

Clog dancing was a strong influence on the development of tap. It probably originated among female woollen mill workers in Lancashire, who tapped out rhythms in wooden clogs to keep time with the **shuttles** of their weaving looms. It was danced purely for the sound, with only the leg below the knee moving. Clog dancing became a popular entertainment, often performed on a slate floor to make the most sound. Competitions were held, which led to the creation of new steps and rhythms.

▼ The metal plates on the soles of tap shoes create the characteristic 'tap' sound in the dancing.

Another forerunner of tap dancing is the hornpipe. This English dance was performed by sailors on sailing ships, in hard shoes that made **percussive** sounds. The dancers would imitate the jobs undertaken on board the ship.

Irish step dancing was taken to the United States by Irish immigrants during the years of the potato famine in the 19th century. Soft shoes were worn for reels and jigs. Hard shoes with wooden heels were worn for heavy jigs, incorporating loud stomping with both heel and toe sounds.

When slaves were transported from Africa to America, they took with them a rich dance tradition that had very different qualities to more formal European dances.

African drumbeats were far more sophisticated than the predictable rhythms of European dances. The drumbeats encouraged swinging, bouncing and hip-swivelling movements. African dancers used a flat rather than a pointed foot, and this is still a feature of modern jazz dance. African dancers would follow different rhythms with different parts of their bodies, a practice called polyrhythmic dancing. In 1739, American law made it illegal for the slaves to use their native drums, so they simply tapped out their rhythms with their feet.

The development of tap

The notorious Five Points district of New York was a site of violent gang crime and slum living conditions, but it was here that tap dancing began. On the streets, Irish immigrants and African Americans engaged in competitive dance battles, blending complex African rhythms and European shoe rhythms. In the nearby Almack's bar, Irish reels and jigs merged with the African American shuffle. It was the beginning of tap dancing.

Amazing Fact

Charlie Chaplin
In the 19th century, clog dancing acts became part of the music hall repertoire. Charlie Chaplin, who later became a star of silent films, was a child member of a clog dancing troupe called The Eight Lancashire Lads.

The term tap dance may have been in use as early as 1900, but it first appeared in writing in 1903.

Tap techniques

Tap dancing gets its name from the sound made by the dancer's shoes on a hard floor, so the performer becomes both dancer and percussive musician. Tap covers a wide range of styles, from informal street dancing to the stage performances of **vaudeville** (see page 22) and film performers such as Fred Astaire.

Tap dancing uses a combination of movements: taps, steps, brushes, shuffles, flaps and **drops** (see box on page 21). Some step names, like **chug** and **rattle**, come from the sounds made, and others from the movements imitated. Other steps are named after the dancers who created them.

The time step was developed to help the dancer communicate the tempo to the band. This was particularly important in the early vaudeville days, as there was often little time for the band and dancer to rehearse together. In the 1930s, individual dancers had their own distinctive time steps. They would usually start a performance with the time step, followed by a set routine or **improvisation**. Today the time step is mostly taught to help dance students develop rhythm.

Tap shoes and clothes

Early tap dancers wore specially constructed split clogs with beech wood soles, designed to give a clear and solid tone. Later, leather tap shoes with iron taps were worn. Tap dancing clothes changed over time, from the frilly shirts and formal tuxedos worn by famous tappers such as the Nicholas Brothers, to the funky street look preferred by modern tapper Gregory Hines.

Dance Facts

Shirley Temple
Child tap star Shirley Temple wore cute tap shoes with large bows tied through the eyelets. This style is still popular for children, but the bows usually have an elastic fastening to prevent them coming undone.

▶ This modern tap troupe is wearing urban style clothing in a show called *Tapdogs Rebooted*.

Technique

Basic steps

Tap: striking either the ball (ball tap) or heel (heel tap) of the foot on the floor.

Step: placing the ball of the foot on the floor and transferring the weight to that foot.

Touch: as above, but without transferring the weight to that foot.

Brush: standing on one leg and sweeping the floor with the ball of the other foot, moving forwards or backwards.

Shuffle: brush forwards and backwards, making two sounds.

Heel drop: standing on the ball of the foot and dropping the heel on to the floor, with one or both feet.

Ball drop: as above, but standing on the heel and dropping the ball.

Flap: a brush forward and a step on the ball of the foot. The heel does not touch the ground and two sounds are made.

More complicated steps, such as paddle and roll, or shuffle ball change, are made by combining these basic steps.

The origins of vaudeville

Today, television provides much of our popular entertainment, but in the days before radio, television or cinema, audiences went to the theatre. In 1880, a family day out might be followed by a trip to the vaudeville variety theatre where musicians, comedians, dancers, acrobats and impersonators performed. The shows were cheap, so they were the perfect place for tap dancing to flourish.

Vaudeville consisted of a programme of short acts or 'turns', each between six and fifteen minutes long. A typical vaudeville programme included a variety of dances. Each act could stand alone, which made it easy to put the programmes together and for performers to travel from theatre to theatre. Travelling between cities was easy as there was a good railway network. This made it easy for tap dancing to reach bigger audiences across the country, and led to a surge in its popularity.

Vaudeville was created for family viewing, and many of the turns were family acts. One of the most famous was The Whitman Sisters. In 1910, the Whitmans took their variety show on the road, travelling to vaudeville theatres with their singers, jazz musicians, comedy routines and dancers. They were renowned for recognizing talent, and nurtured many new artists who later became stars of stage and screen.

Famous Dancers

King Rastus Brown

King Rastus Brown was an early pioneer of tap dance. He was a versatile dancer who danced with his body bent forward, using the flat-footed style that had its roots in African dancing. As well as tap, he danced the Irish jig, the cakewalk, and the **sand dance**, and performed with a cane. He was renowned for his abilities as an imitator, and would respond to requests from the audience to impersonate other dancers.

Famous Dancers

Clayton 'Peg Leg' Bates (1907–98)

One of the most impressive tap dancers of his generation, Clayton Bates proved that it was possible to achieve high standards of tap with only one leg. Bates started dancing as a child, but in 1918 he had his leg amputated below the knee after a horrific accident with a machine. He was determined to continue dancing, and after his uncle made him a peg leg he was soon dancing again.

A popular performer, Bates appeared on 22 episodes of the *Ed Sullivan Show*, on which he amazed audiences with his **rhythm tap** and novelty steps, leaps and balances.

▼ These vaudeville dancers performed their act as part of the show.

The silver screen

In the late 1920s, new technology allowed the development of the 'talkie', a film with sound. By 1929 all Hollywood films were made with sound. Films had been included in the **vaudeville** programmes, but now cinema became the most popular form of entertainment. In the 1930s, 1940s, and 1950s, the best tap dancers moved from vaudeville to films and television.

Famous Dancers

Steve Condos (1918–90)
Rhythm tap legend Steve Condos was one performer who successfully made the transition from vaudeville to screen. With his brother Nick he performed as one of the Condos Brothers. They were known for their tricky footwork and complicated steps. Later, as a tap soloist, Steve experimented with **percussive** rhythms that amazed and impressed both critics and dancers. As one observer put it, 'All he cared about was the music of his feet. The upper body meant nothing to him. His feet told the story'. Condos appeared in more than 40 films.

Hoofers Club

Many hopefuls in New York's Harlem district aspired to be tap dancing stars in films. From the 1920s to the 1940s, the Hoofers Club was an important venue for nurturing new tap dancing talent. Many of the tap dancing greats of the period made their debut in this unglamorous setting of a small back room in Harlem. A set of strict rules were operated by the club owner, Lonnie Hicks: you could only have access to the club if you were going to dance; dancers were not permitted to perform another dancer's steps for money; and stealing steps was considered a serious offence.

Close by the Hoofers Club, an old elm tree grew. Known as the tree of hope, many believed that if you touched or kissed the bark of the tree your wishes would come true. Dancers performed and practised new moves around the tree, hoping to become the hottest new star of stage and screen.

Famous Dancers

Bill 'Bojangles' Robinson (1878–1949)

Bill 'Bojangles' Robinson was a star of **Broadway**, and also had 16 films to his credit. His dance style was cool and relaxed, emphasizing leg movements and facial expressions. Like the earlier dancers, he did not make use of his hands or include much body motion. His dancing had a light quality and precise rhythmic timing. He is credited with 'moving tap up on to its toes', away from the flat-footed style that was common at the time. His unique contribution to tap dancing was the famous stair dance, which involved tapping up and down a flight of stairs so that each step reverberated at a different pitch.

Bill 'Bojangles' Robinson danced in 16 films. Most frequently he took the role of a butler, but he also played the mayor of Harlem in *One Step from Heaven*.

Fred and Ginger

The films of the 1930s heralded a new age for tap dancing. This was a glamorous, elegant era, epitomized by the dancing duo Fred Astaire and Ginger Rogers.

Fred and Ginger were the image of grace and Hollywood glamour. They were possibly the most famous male/female tap dancing partnership of all time. Fred Astaire, dressed in a smart tuxedo and top hat, gave tap the elegance of ballroom dancing. Ginger Rogers wore floating dresses trimmed with beads and feathers that made the dance look effortless as she glided around the floor. They had an onscreen chemistry that appealed to cinema audiences.

▶ The magical partnership of Fred Astaire and Ginger Rogers spanned six years, from 1933 to 1939. This is the musical number 'Pick Yourself Up' from the film *Swing Time*.

Fred Astaire

Astaire started dancing in vaudeville, partnered by his sister Adele. When that partnership ended, he made a screen test and was taken on by RKO Pictures. It was in his second film, *Flying Down to Rio* (1933), that he made innovations that changed the way dance was shown on film. In the early days of dance on film, real live shows were filmed from the viewpoint of someone sitting in the auditorium of a theatre. Dancing was filmed, but the camera would cut away to show the feet, then to a smiling face, or to someone clapping in the audience. Fred Astaire insisted that the dance should be filmed in its entirety, with no cutaway. He also insisted that all the song and dance routines should be integrated into the plot lines, to move the story along, and not used purely for spectacle. Typically, a Fred Astaire film would include a solo performance, a partnered comedy routine and a partnered romantic dance routine.

Astaire's background in ballroom dancing helped to shape his dance style, which he called 'outlaw style'. This style is recognized by the sudden change from flowing movements to abrupt stops. Cholly Atkins described the quality of Astaire's performance in this way: 'He used balletic turns but came out of them with a jazz kick and slide.'

Ginger Rogers

Over the years, Astaire danced with many partners but his most popular pairing was with Ginger Rogers. Rogers' career also started in vaudeville. She then had a film contract with Paramount, before she teamed up with Astaire in *Flying Down to Rio*.

Rogers was not the greatest dancer, but her abilities as an actress and comedienne, as well as her elegant style, complemented Astaire's talents. Astaire himself commented that 'after a while everyone else who danced with me looked wrong'. Their ten-film partnership included many fine dance routines, but the highlight is generally thought to be 'A Waltz in Swing Time', from the 1936 film *Swing Time*. Critics consider this the finest partnered dance performed by Astaire.

The silver screen

Fred Astaire used film to capture a performance of a dance as it would be seen by an audience in a theatre. At the same time, musical producer Busby Berkeley had a very different idea: he wanted to use clever camerawork to show cinema audiences dance performances as they had never been seen before.

Cinematic style: Busby Berkeley (1895–1976)

With fantasy elements, geometric patterns, elaborate costumes and staging, Busby Berkeley's musical productions are instantly recognizable. In complete contrast to the straightforward camerawork in a Fred Astaire dance scene, Berkeley deliberately used unusual angles. This new cinema perspective was quite unlike watching a theatrical performance.

▲ Busby Berkeley introduced these geometric patterns to his musical productions.

The typical sequence of a Berkeley musical number would start with a shot of a stage, then move into a series of cinematic scenes. The sequence would end with a return to the stage set, usually with the fall of a curtain and an applauding audience. Berkeley's techniques included the 'parade of faces', which gave individual identities to the women in the chorus line; the top shot, which showed a scene shot from overhead; and the kaleidoscope effect, which created images like those seen through a child's kaleidoscope.

Berkeley's groundbreaking film *42nd Street* (1933) is about putting on a show. Set during the **Depression** of the late 1920s, it followed in the tradition of the 'backstage musical' and was a gritty look at the realities of backstage life. It was quite unlike the glamorous Astaire and Rogers films of the same period. Twenty minutes of footage devoted to three Berkeley numbers ('Shuffle off to Buffalo', 'I'm Young and Healthy' and '42nd Street') showcased the new Berkeley techniques.

Famous Dancers

Little Darlin' Shirley Temple (born 1928)

In the gloomy years of the Depression, one dancing star brought joy to cinema audiences. With her blonde bubble curls, dimpled smile and unaffected cuteness, Shirley Temple was extremely popular.

Temple was born in California, USA, in 1928. When she was just three years old she enrolled at the Ethel Meglin Dance Studios, where she learned to tap dance. By the time she was four, she was earning ten dollars a day and by 1935 she was the number one box office star. Between 1934 and 1940, Temple made an astonishing 24 films, of which 15 included tap dance sequences. She danced with the greatest stars of the day, most memorably with Bill 'Bojangles' Robinson.

Shirley Temple made tap dance a popular pastime. Each time a new Temple film was released, enrolment figures at dance classes rose dramatically. People believed that if Shirley could tap at just three years old, it was possible for anyone to do.

▶ Shirley Temple tap dances with Bill 'Bojangles' Robinson in *The Littlest Rebel*, 1935.

A dancing spectacle

The elegant and stylish performances of Astaire's and Berkeley's routines are in contrast to the acrobatic **flash dancing** of the Nicholas Brothers, and Gene Kelly's informal signature dance style.

The Nicholas Brothers

The Nicholas Brothers, Fayard Nicholas and Harold Nicholas, were unsurpassed for their flash dancing, a fusion of jazz, tap dance and acrobatics. *Who's Who in Hollywood* described them as 'the greatest dance team ever to work in the movies'.

Their routine for 'Down Argentine Way', choreographed by Nick Castle, featured ten-foot leaps straight into the splits. Castle choreographed their most dangerous stunt, which Fayard described: 'He had us take a long run, climb up a wall for two full steps, and backflip, no hands, into a split, bouncing up from a split on the beat.'

In the 1940s, the brothers made six films for 20th Century Fox, including their personal favourite, *Stormy Weather* (1943). This was based loosely on the life of Bill 'Bojangles' Robinson and featured the Brothers' signature stunt: dancing down a long broad flight of steps, leapfrogging over each other and landing in a complete split on each step.

The Nicholas Brothers received many awards for their work. Fayard was given a Tony Award for his choreography of the Broadway show *Black and Blue* in 1989, and Harold was given the Harbor Performing Arts Center Lifetime Achievement Award.

Famous Dancers

One of a kind: Jeni LeGon (born 1916)

Unlike most female tap dancers of her generation, Jeni LeGon achieved success as a female solo artist dancing in trousers and low heels, instead of the usual skirts and high heels. Her routines included splits, flips and toe stands – flash work that was usually only done by male dancers.

Gene Kelly

In the 1940s, Gene Kelly developed a more informal style of dance. He is best remembered splashing in puddles and swinging around lamp posts in *Singin' in the Rain* (1952), and tap dancing in roller skates in *It's Always Fair Weather* (1953).

Kelly's big film break came in 1944, when he starred opposite Rita Hayworth in *Cover Girl*. Kelly had artistic control of the film and introduced several new ideas. For example, he used trick photography so that he could dance with his own reflection in one sequence. By superimposing one image on another he was able to give his double a ghost-like appearance.

Kelly's dance style was athletic, with a grace derived from his early ballet training. His casual costumes suited his energetic dancing, and this informality appealed to cinema audiences of the day.

▲ Gene Kelly co-directed, choreographed, and starred in *An American in Paris* (1951) and *Singin' in the Rain* (1952, seen here). In 1951, Kelly was presented with an honorary Academy Award for his contribution to film musicals and choreography.

Theatrical jazz

During the 1950s, a new demanding style of dance emerged that came to be known as modern or theatrical jazz. It was a mix of ballet and modern dance, created by choreographers with a background in both styles.

Jack Cole

One of these choreographers, Jack Cole (1911–74), was known as the 'father of theatrical jazz'. He developed a style of dance that is recognizable in musicals and films from the 1950s to the present day. Cole was an innovator, combining many different dance forms in a style that influenced many future choreographers, such as Jerome Robbins, Bob Fosse, Gwen Verdon, and George Balanchine.

Technique

Typical moves

Barrel jump: jump with both legs bent back from the knee and both arms up, in any basic pose.

Jazz run: running jazz walk requiring grace and balance to make it look natural.

Jazz square: four-step movement in which a dancer steps out on the right leg, steps back with the left leg, crosses over with the right leg, and steps forward with the left leg, creating a full square.

Kick: a high kick, throwing up the leg in a controlled manner.

Pencil turn: a spin on both feet keeping the body straight – the body spins a few times with ease.

Shimmie: one shoulder moves forward while the other moves back really fast in a shake.

Stag leap: a high leap or jump in a split but with the front leg bent inward from the knee.

Modern or theatrical jazz is a highly flexible dance form, which is often taught in dance schools and fused with other dance styles. It is based on ballet technique, which is used to strengthen the body and improve balance. Unlike earlier forms of jazz dance, it requires high levels of formal training and is based on choreographed routines.

Famous Dancers

Jerome Robbins (1918–98)
Robbins studied a wide range of dance styles, including ballet, modern dance, Spanish dance, folk dance and dance composition. In 1957, he choreographed *West Side Story*, a contemporary version of *Romeo and Juliet* set in the New York neighbourhood of Hell's Kitchen. The musical score by Leonard Bernstein combined a big band jazz sound with Latin mambo. The choreography was energetic and was used with music and costume to distinguish the different ethnic backgrounds of the two gangs. In the famous Jets and Sharks confrontation scene, the escalating violence is expressed through a **crescendo**, which starts with a single clicking finger and **syncopated** rhythm, building to a full big band sound. The accompanying choreography starts with a cruising pace and ends with a frenzy. *West Side Story* is widely regarded as Robbins' finest achievement.

Jerome Robbins created a blend of dance and stage action in *West Side Story*. Dancers in the Jets and Sharks gangs were kept apart in rehearsals, to help build the tension between them.

▲ Ben Vereen plays O'Connor Flood in the 1979 film of Bob Fosse's *All That Jazz*.

Bob Fosse and musical theatre

In the second half of the 20th century, musical theatre continued to develop. In this period, innovator Bob Fosse (1927–87) made a distinctive contribution to jazz dance style.

The main influences on Bob Fosse's work were Jack Cole's theatrical jazz and Jerome Robbins' choreography. Trademarks of Fosse's stylized choreography include the use of inward knee thrusts, protruding hips, rounded shoulders and wrist movements.

Typical Fosse movements include the head roll, in which the head moves in a complete circle by rotating the neck, while the body remains in an upright position. The movement is both controlled and relaxed. He also introduced hand roll movements. Fosse admired Fred Astaire, and developed his own use of hats and gloves.

Fosse introduced the idea of **subtext** by asking his dancers to think about specific things that would affect their interpretation of a musical number. He also developed a theatrical style that made use of dramatic spot lighting to draw attention to important actions.

Fosse as director

Fosse wrote and directed *All That Jazz* (1979), which was based loosely on his life as a dancer and choreographer. He directed four other films, including *Cabaret* (1972). Set in 1930s Berlin, *Cabaret* tells the story of Sally Bowles (played by Liza Minnelli), an aspiring singer in the Kit Kat club. *Cabaret* began as a **Broadway** production, and in the transition from stage to screen Fosse made some important changes:

- He gave the film a dark theatrical treatment, influenced by **vaudeville** and **burlesque**, which suited the subject.
- He added a harshly made-up master of ceremonies as commentator on the story, which increased the tension.
- He removed all the songs that were sung outside the Kit Kat club, and introduced several new songs.
- The music was played by a stage band within the film, rather than an unseen orchestra.

▼ In this 2006 stage production of *Cabaret*, Sally Bowles was played by Anna Maxwell Martin.

New directions

Towards the end of the 1940s, tap dancing declined in popularity. Many reasons have been suggested for this, including the emergence of rock and roll. Another factor was the evolution of jazz music, from the big bands of the 1930s to the small combos of the late 1940s and 1950s. While the 1930s bands had played music that was sympathetic to tap dancing, the irregular rhythms of bebop drummers, dropping beats in unexpected places, made tap accompaniment more challenging.

While rock and roll ruled in the clubs and dance halls, tap and jazz were having a hard time on stage and film. Perhaps audiences had become too used to tap dance, and were no longer excited by it. In film, Agnes de Mille's choreography of the film *Oklahoma!* (1955) marked a move to a more balletic form of dance, while George Balanchine's choreography of musicals led a move away from jazz dance into a ballet-inspired style.

In the 1950s and 1960s, jazz dance continued to evolve in new directions. Danny Buraczeski called the form a 'melting pot of countless styles and influences'. Cholly Atkins was involved in the transformation of jazz in the new popular music scene.

Famous Dancers

Ann Miller (1923–2004)
Following in the footsteps of tap greats Ruby Keeler and Eleanor Powell, Ann Miller was the tap star of films such as *Easter Parade* (1948), *On the Town* (1949) and *Kiss Me Kate* (1953). Her energetic dance style was in the 'hoofer' tradition, rather than the choreographed acrobatics of Eleanor Powell. She was known as the woman with the 'machine-gun' taps and was hailed in Ripley's 'Believe it, or Not' as the world's fastest tap dancer. With a speedometer attached to her feet she achieved a phenomenal 500 taps a minute.

Gladys Knight and the Pips were one of the Motown groups to be given the Cholly Atkins treatment. This performance was in 1968.

Vocal choreography: Cholly Atkins

Cholly Atkins (1913–2003) was responsible for transforming jazz into a form that endured until the 1990s. Early in his career, he watched choreographers at work in film studios and learned about producing and directing. From 1965 to 1971 he worked for the Motown record company, where his job was to transform streetwise hit makers into live performers, by choreographing steps to match their songs. The problem, he remarked, was that 'everybody was moving, but they were doing whatever they felt like doing'. His job was to organize them to create a more precise dance form. He used moves from modern jazz, ballet moves, or jazz tap moves without the taps. The **vocal choreography** style that Atkins developed included tap moves such as cross steps, over-the-tops and trenches, all done in a jazz style. So, working with groups such as Gladys Knight and the Pips, The Supremes, The Miracles and The Temptations, Cholly Atkins can be credited with keeping American jazz dance alive through the medium of popular music.

Looking back, facing forward: the revivals

In the 1970s and 1980s, dancers and choreographers looked back to the jazz dance styles of the early 20th century for inspiration. Ragtime music became popular again in the 1970s following the use of Scott's Joplin's 'The Entertainer' as the score for the film *The Sting* (1973). Kenneth Macmillan, director of The Royal Ballet, used Joplin's music for his ballet, *Elite Syncopations*, in which dancers in brightly-coloured costumes compete against each other while dancing to Scott Joplin's bouncing **syncopated** rhythms. In the same period, two more ballets were choreographed for ragtime music: Alfonso Catá's *Ragtime*, performed by the Frankfurt Ballet, and a two-act piece, *Prodigal Son*, choreographed by Barry Moreland for the London Festival Ballet.

Swing revival

The early 1980s swing revival led to the formation of Rhythm Hot Shots, a Swedish dance company specializing in the reproduction of dance scenes in American films of the swing era. The group tracked down original swing dancers from the 1930s and 1940s to teach its members more about their dance techniques. Their search led them to lindy hop legend Frankie Manning, who agreed to teach them. In 1984, two American dancers, Steven Mitchell and Erin Stevens, also visited Manning and within a year the lindy hop revival was in full swing. Veteran lindy hoppers Al Minns and Norma Miller came out of retirement to join Manning in training the new generation of dancers.

Night clubs began to feature swing dance nights. Bands such as Royal Crown Revue, Big Bad Voodoo Daddy and the Brian Setzer Orchestra gave swing music a modern twist. Swing became cool again, with films such as *Swing Kids* (1993) and *Swingers* (1996) celebrating swing dance, music and lifestyle.

In 1998, advertising picked up the theme when Gap filmed a commercial using lindy hoppers dancing in khakis to a classic Louis Prima hit 'Jump Jive an' Wail', performed by the Brian Setzer Orchestra. New digital film techniques were used to exaggerate the aerial steps, and give the impression that the dancers were suspended in mid-air.

Famous Dancers

Gregory Hines (1946–2003)
Tap also had a revival, championed by dancer Gregory Hines. Hines started dancing with his father and older brother, Maurice, in The Hines Kids. He went on to become an actor and dancer working in film, television and theatre. Hines performed in the film *The Cotton Club* (1984), in which he danced Bill Robinson's famous staircase dance. Footage of Robinson's original dance was seamlessly blended with footage of Hines dancing. Hines was a lifelong advocate of tap dance, and he successfully lobbied for the creation of a National Tap Dance Day in the United States, which is 25th May.

▲ Gregory Hines starred in *The Cotton Club* (1984), *White Nights* (1985), *Tap* (1989, seen here) and *Bojangles* (2001).

Modern jazz dance theatre

While Hines and the new generation of lindy hoppers were looking back to the early 20th century, other dancers were developing new styles merging jazz with modern dance, ballet or Latin dance. New dance styles emphasized natural movement, with rhythm regarded as more important than set positions and steps.

Gus Giordano

Gus Giordano (1923–2008) was a key figure in modern jazz dance. An influential teacher and founder of the annual Jazz Dance World Congress, Giordano was influenced by Jelly Roll Morton's music. He studied African dance with Katherine Dunham and modern dance with pioneer Hanya Holm.

Giordano was an innovator in jazz dance, and introduced new waving movements through the pelvis, chest and arms. In the 1970s, Giordano compiled a book about his technique and teaching style. This book has since become one of the most influential books on the subject and has helped to shape contemporary jazz dance. He also wrote a two-volume history of American **social dance**.

Alvin Ailey

Alvin Ailey (1931–89) continued the evolution of jazz dance, borrowing from other dance styles and blending them in original forms. Among the influences that fed into Ailey's unique jazz style were the African dance style of the Katherine Dunham Dance Company, the Ballet Russe de Monte Carlo, and Martha Graham's modern dance technique. Ailey trained formally with Lester Horton, whose style included Native American and Japanese influences with modern jazz, emphasizing freedom of movement and flexibility. He studied ballet and was also taught by Martha Graham, a pioneer of modern dance.

Ailey's dance style drew on the blues, spirituals and gospel as inspiration. It was concerned with the African American experience. His choreography for *Blues Suite* (1958), set in a **barrelhouse**, depicts the ups and downs of life in the Deep South of the United States. The dance draws on the social dances of the early 20th century, Jack Cole jazz technique and ballet. It was followed in 1960 by *Revelations* and *Feast of Ashes* (1962).

In 1970, Ailey created *The River,* set to a score commissioned from Duke Ellington. The ballet mixed theatrical jazz dance with ballet. In the same year, his dance company became the first American dance company to tour the Soviet Union for 50 years.

▼ The Alvin Ailey Dance Theater combines popular music, gospel, and jazz in this production at Sadler's Wells theatre in 2007.

Technique

Modern jazz dance moves

Dolphin or snake: the body flows in a snake-like movement, starting from the chest and moving up.

Ripple: a snake-like movement that starts at the pelvis and works its way up to the torso, moving in either direction.

Contraction: a basic modern movement where the dancer contracts the mid section.

Arch: the opposite of a contraction. The mid section pushes forward and the back arches.

Where are we now?

After three decades in which musical theatre has been the main focus of tap and jazz, jazz dance is renewing itself. Street dance is returning to its roots, with dancers competing against each other just as the early jazz dancers in New Orleans and Harlem did.

Jazz dance today

Jazz dance, having been pushed underground by disco, is undergoing a rebirth. As world dance styles have become more popular, jazz has merged with the funky rhythms of Brazilian, Cuban and Latin music, resulting in street fusion jazz. This style focuses on leg movements and footwork with acrobatic techniques, such as the drop move, in which the dancer drops to the floor and takes up a controlled position.

JazzCotech, founded by Perry Louis, is a UK-based street fusion jazz company. The dancers are selected from a clubbing background and most have no formal dance training, just like the Savoy dancers years before. The group has performed with artists such as James Brown and Jamiroquai.

▼ JazzCotech is an innovative street fusion jazz company.

Famous Dancers

Body percussion: stomp

Stomp is a show that was first seen in Brighton in 1991. It has given its name to a form of dance featuring energetic rhythmic combinations of body percussion, movement and comedy. The show was created by musicians Luke Cresswell and Steve McNicholas, and uses everyday objects such as brooms, bins, bananas and boxes of matches to make percussive noise. A film of the show, *Stomp Out Loud* (1997), was made in the back streets of Manhattan in New York City.

▼ Urban influences are seen in *Stomp*, which uses everyday objects to create percussive sounds.

Billy Siegenfeld's Jump Rhythm Jazz Project, founded in Chicago in 1993, emphasizes moving the body to the **syncopated** rhythms of beat driven music. *Dancer* magazine credited Siegenfeld with 'inventing the first genuine jazz technique in forty years'. Jump rhythm jazz is a high energy approach, focusing on using the body as a **percussion** instrument, and emphasizing rhythm above other dance elements.

Tap today

Tap dancing styles have also been given a modern twist. In 2000, the Tap Dogs opened the Olympic Games in Sydney. The group, led by Australian choreographer Dein Perry, demonstrated a dazzling array of skills. Tap Dogs is credited with revolutionizing modern tap dance.

The future

Jazz and tap are versatile forms, capable of constant reinvention. As choreographer Bob Boross puts it: 'Jazz takes shape in techniques that have withstood the test of time. From its folk origins and the innovations of the masters, to the work of today's classic and contemporary artists, jazz dance lives in the techniques, styles, and personalities of many practitioners.'

Timeline

Jazz and tap dance emerged in late 19th-century America from the fusion of African, Irish, and English dances. Since then, this versatile dance form has developed into many different dance styles. Here is a brief history of key moments in the development of jazz dance:

1844 Rivals William Henry Lane and John Diamond engage in a series of challenge dances.

1900s–1910s – Ragtime and early jazz

1900 The turkey trot is danced to Scott Joplin's 'Maple Leaf Rag'.

1907 *The Ziegfeld Follies* opens. The revue-style show nurtures future dance stars such as Barbara Stanwyck and Paulette Goddard.

1913 Vernon and Irene Castle perform the turkey trot in the **Broadway** show, *The Sunshine Girl*.

1914 Harry Fox performs the foxtrot on the roof of the New York Theater.

1920s – The birth of swing

In the early swing era, jazz dance is both a **social dance** and a performance dance. Dances that develop in the ballrooms are incorporated into Broadway musicals.

1923 The Charleston is performed in *Runnin' Wild* and becomes a dance sensation.

1924 The black bottom is performed in the show *Dinah*, and soon replaces the Charleston as the popular dance of the day.

1925 On 2 October Josephine Baker dances the Charleston in her show *La Revue Nègre* at Théâtre des Champs Élysées in Paris. This is the height of the jazz age in Paris.

1927 The lindy hop develops in New York. Lindy hop is both a solo and a partnered dance, which blends European partner dancing with the movements and **improvisations** of African dance.

1930s – Glamour in the Depression

Film becomes increasingly important in the development of jazz dance.

1933 Fred Astaire choreographs and dances in *Flying Down to Rio*. Astaire insists that dance sequences are filmed with no cutaway to the feet, face, or audience.

1933 Busby Berkeley's groundbreaking *42nd Street* uses a chorus line, unusual angles and kaleidoscopic images and other new techniques.

1935 Shirley Temple and Bill 'Bojangles' Robinson co-star in *The Little Colonel*. Bill Robinson dances his famous tap sequence on the stairs.

1935 Meanwhile in the ballrooms social dance is also developing. Benny Goodman's new jazz music performed at the Palomar Ballroom leads to the development of a new improvised dance style – the **jitterbug**.

1940s – Flash acts and casual charm

Jazz and tap dance continue to feature in Hollywood films. Dance styles vary from the **flash dance** acts of the Nicholas Brothers and Jeni LeGon, to the graceful balletic style of Gene Kelly.

1940 Fayard and Harold Nicholas perform in *Down Argentine Way*. Their flash act routine is full of spectacular and dangerous acrobatic sequences.

1944 Gene Kelly stars in *Cover Girl* opposite Rita Hayworth. He introduces special effects that create the illusion that he is dancing with his reflection.

1950s – Theatrical jazz

In the 1950s, a new dance style, theatrical jazz, combines elements of ballet and modern dance. Jack Cole is a choreographer at Columbia Pictures. His innovations influence a whole generation.

1957 Jerome Robbins choreographs *West Side Story*. The musical score fuses big band jazz with Latin mambo. Robbins' energetic choreography is used to contrast the ethnic backgrounds of the rival gangs, the Sharks and Jets.

1960s–70s – Surviving rock and roll

By the end of the 1950s jazz dance is under threat from rock and roll, followed by disco in the 1960s and 70s. Jazz survives in the theatre and finds a new outlet in Cholly Atkins' **vocal choreography**.

1964 Berry Gordy employs Cholly Atkins to add polish and class to the artists performing under the Motown music label. He works with Marvin Gaye, Gladys Knight and the Pips, and The Supremes among others.

1973 Kenneth Macmillan uses Scott Joplin's music 'The Entertainer' for his ballet *Elite Syncopations*.

1975 Bob Fosse choreographs the Broadway musical *Chicago*, introducing new jazz movements, the idea of **subtext**, and the dramatic use of spotlighting.

1980s – Jazz dance revivals

Dancers and choreographers look back to the jazz dance styles of the early 20th century.

1984 Gregory Hines stars in *The Cotton Club*, in which he reproduces Bill Robinson's staircase dance with footage from Robinson's original dance blended with his own.

1985 Dance group Rhythm Hot Shots are formed, specialising in the revival of lindy hop and other jazz and swing dances.

1990s onwards – New directions

Jazz and tap continue to thrive, with street and global influences shaping the new dance styles. Perry Louis founds the JazzCotech Dancers, a UK street fusion dance style known as Old Skool Jazz Dance.

1991 The show *Stomp* is first seen in Brighton.

1993 Billy Siegenfeld's Jump Rhythm Jazz Project is founded. His technique emphasises rhythm and uses the body to make **percussive** sounds.

2000 Dance group Tap Dogs perform at the opening ceremony of the Olympic Games in Sydney.

Glossary

barrelhouse disreputable old-time saloon or bar; also the name of an early style of jazz characterised by boisterous piano playing

Broadway street in New York City that runs the length of Manhattan and is closely associated with the theatre

burlesque risqué and bawdy variety show featuring comedy and dancing

chug term used for specific footwork: a sharp movement (usually backwards) of the supporting foot or feet where the foot or feet does not leave the floor

close hold when dance partners stand close together in physical contact

crescendo when music increases in volume until maximum intensity is reached

Depression the Great Depression in 1930s America was a period of deprivation

Dixieland jazz style of jazz originating in New Orleans, USA. It is sometimes called Hot Jazz. It combined brass band music with ragtime, blues, and French Quadrilles.

drop tap dance move. There are two basic drop steps: ball drop and heel drop.

eight-count call used to count the rhythm of foot movements or the beats of the music: eight-count is eight beats; two-count is two-beats; four-count is four beats; six-count is six beats

flapper term used in the 1920s to describe young women who dressed in shorter skirts, wore bobbed hairstyles, and listened and danced to jazz music

flash dancing impressive style of jazz dance that uses flash steps. These are acrobatic movements.

gilly travelling form of entertainment named after the decorated trucks used to transport the show from one town to the next

harmonically in music harmony is the structure, the relationships between chords and notes. Harmonically is an adjective meaning in a harmonious manner.

hoecake bread made from cornmeal. It is unleavened, which means it is a flatbread made without yeast.

improvisation unplanned elements in a performance

jitterbug energetic dance performed to quick-tempo, embellished with twirls and sometimes acrobatic manoeuvres

lyrical expressive and emotional

medicine shows travelling shows at which peddlars would sell medicines and miracle cures. A dancer might be used to attract an audience.

off-beat term applied to music where the rhythm accentuates the weaker beats in the bar. Dancing on the off-beat similarly is executing steps on the unstressed beats.

one-step simple and easily learned dance, sometimes called 'the walking step' because it was done at a brisk walking step executed to each beat of the music

percussion the creation of sound by tapping, scraping, and beating

precursor something that comes earlier than the thing that is mentioned

rattle tap step named after the rattling sound that is produced

rhythm tap when the rhythms that the feet make are the most important element of the dance

sand dance dance, popular in music halls, that parodied Egyptian movements and Arabic costumes

shuttle device used in weaving to carry the woven thread back and forth horizontally between the vertical threads

social dances dances where the main focus is socialising. Other dance categories are ethnic and performance.

subtext the story within the story, often implicit rather than explicit

syncopated in dance syncopation is used in two different ways: 1) stepping on an unstressed beat and 2) step patterns that are rhythmically more complex than standard step patterns. West Coast Swing is a syncopated dance style in this sense of the word.

two-step dance move consisting of two steps in approximately the same direction onto the same foot, separated by a closing step with the other foot

vaudeville form of theatrical entertainment that emerged in 19th-century America. Similar to music hall, vaudeville was a family show consisting of a number of variety acts such as juggler, comedian, dancer, and acrobat.

vernacular language native to a country or region

vocal choreography choreographed dance steps that accompany songs

further information

Books

Frankie Manning: Ambassador of Lindy Hop, Frankie Manning and Cynthia Millman (Temple University Press, 2007)

Jazz Dance, Marshall and Jean Stearns (Da Capo Press, 1994)

Steppin' on the Blues: The Visible Rhythms of African American Dance, Jacqui Malone (Illinois University Press, 1996)

Tap Dancing: Rhythm in Their Feet, Heather Rees (Crowood Press, 2003)

Tap Roots: The Early History of Tap Dancing, Mark Knowles (McFarland, 2002)

Tap! The Greatest Tap Dance Stars and Their Stories, 1900–1955, Rusty Frank (Da Capo Press, 1994)

Films

Hellzapoppin' (1941)
Singin' in the Rain (1952)
West Side Story (1961)
Cabaret (1972)
The Cotton Club (1984)
Tap (1989)

Websites

www.alvinailey.org/
Alvin Ailey American Dance Theater.

www.jazzcotech.com/
JazzCotech Dancers, the UK jazz dance group.

www.savoystyle.com/
The archives of early lindy hop.

www.fosse.com/
The life and work of Bob Fosse.

www.jazzdanceworldcongress.org/
Jazz Dance World Congress, the international annual celebration of jazz dance.

Index